Copyright © 2022 Red Whit

All rights reserved

The characters and events portrayed in this book are fictitious. Any similarity to real persons, living or dead, is coincidental and not intended by the author.

No part of this book may be reproduced, or stored in a retrieval system, or transmitted in any form or by any means, electronic, mechanical, photocopying, recording, or otherwise, without express written permission of the publisher.

I dedicate this collection of books to my grandchildren and all inquisitive children everywhere.

I thank my family for checking and reviewing them for me.

BOOK #1 - THE VANISHING SUN INCIDENT

In which, the Sun disappears, causing some major changes to people's lives.

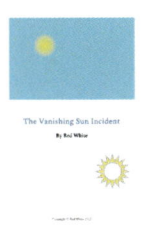

THE VANISHING SUN INCIDENT

By Red White

DAY 1 - THE DAY THAT THE SUN VANISHED

It was a normal, happy day in Anytown, Anywhere. Zen and Zelda woke up, hopped out of bed, raced for the bathroom, then dressed and went downstairs for breakfast. Zen had wheat cereal and strawberries. His sister Zelda tucked into rice cereal and bananas.

It was still dark when they left the house, which was odd, because it was Spring and it should have been sunny. It was chillier than yesterday, or the day before that. Luckily, the streetlights had stayed on, so they could find their way to school safely.

At morning break time they went outside to find that it was still dark. There were no clouds, so where was the Sun? The teacher decided that they should go back inside for everyone's safety, as there might be a big storm coming, so they did.

At lunchtime it was still dark and everybody started to be a little bit worried. Where had the Sun gone? The teacher turned the television on and tuned it to the Serious Education Channel. A serious looking announcer was interviewing an even more serious looking lady scientist who was pointing to a diagram of the Solar System, which is where the Earth is.

"The Sun should be right here, at the center of our Solar System", she said, pointing to the diagram. "This morning it just disappeared. There is no sunlight anywhere in the World."

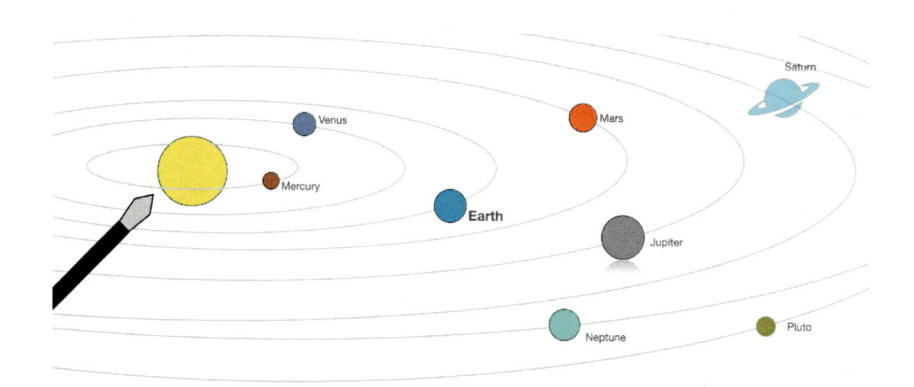

"But don't all the planets go around the Sun, held in orbit by gravity?", asked the interviewer? "If it's gone, won't we all fly off into Outer Space?"

"Yes, in theory," said the scientist, "as that is what we would expect. However, we haven't left our regular orbit. There must be something extremely heavy where the Sun was, or maybe the Sun has simply stopped glowing. We have always expected that to happen one day, but not for billions of years. We have satellites near the Sun, so we should know which it is soon."

"What can people do?", asked the interviewer. "Do we need to stock up on food and water and things?" The Scientist paused - "I'd wait until we know exactly what is going on", she replied. "We shouldn't panic and buy things that we might never need, as it could make things hard for other people who really need something for a special reason."

DAY 2 - PEOPLE START TO WONDER

The children woke a bit late the next day. There was still no sign of the Sun and the morning news programs were all talking about the situation. There were multiple ideas, such as the one that aliens from Outer Space had blown up the Sun, or put a gigantic screen between us and it.

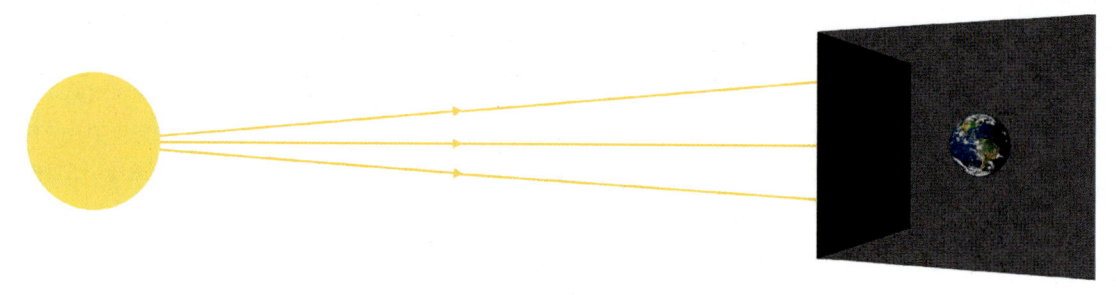

Another group thought that a giant space serpent had swallowed it whole and was now curled up in the middle of the Solar System.

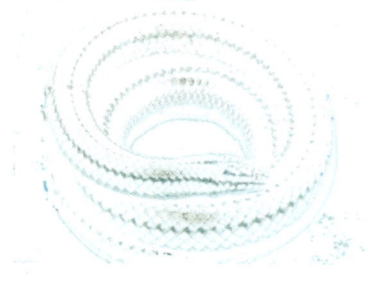

Many people blamed people in faraway places they'd never visited but feared for some reason. Some people thought that it was a sign that the end of everything was near. One person who said he was a scientist, but turned out to be a magic water salesman, thought that the Sun had always been flat and thin and had simply flipped over on its back.

The children went off to school as usual, hoping that the Sun would soon come back. Their teacher told them that in the very Northern and Southern parts of the Earth it is quite normal to go months without seeing the Sun at all. Then in the Summer the Sun is up all day, so there is no night time for months.

In those areas, they can't grow much food in the winter as plants and trees need sunlight. So they have created indoor farms that use water instead of soil, a special plant food and electric lights that produce the same colors that the Sun does. They also buy a lot of food from nearby countries that have plenty of sunlight all year. The problem now was that no countries had any sunlight.

DAY 3 - THE ANIMALS AND BIRDS START BEHAVING STRANGELY

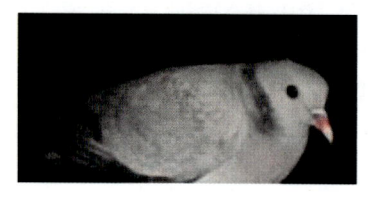

It was strangely quiet when Zen and Zelda woke up. It took a while before Zen suddenly said "Where are the birds? Our robin isn't chirping and neither are the turtle doves." His mother said that she thought that they might still be asleep, as birds roost at night, either in their nests or perched on tree branches. Zen ran upstairs to check out the robin's nest. He shone a flashlight on it. Sure enough, there she was, curled up asleep, though she sleepily opened one eye, so Zen turned off the light.

Father drove them to school that morning, as Mother had a breakfast meeting with her friends. They were all shocked when Father braked suddenly. A family of badgers was crossing the road in front of them. The frightened creatures stopped to stare at the car headlights, so Father turned the main ones off for a moment so that the little animals would get across the road safely. Once the badgers were gone they carried on to school, eager to tell their friends about it.

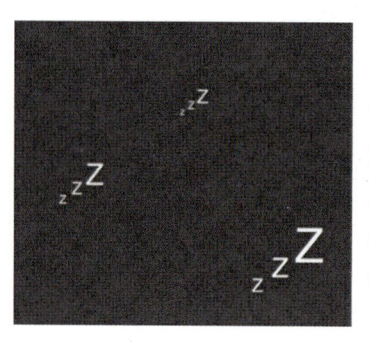

"My dog, Zeta, didn't want to get up this morning", said Zelda's friend Zarah after she'd been told about the birds and badgers. "I wonder what animals that normally forage for fruit or berries, or hunt for food in the daytime are going to do? Will we keep seeing owls and badgers at odd times during the day, or hear other animals snoring in the bushes?"

WEEK 1 - THE PLANTS START CHANGING

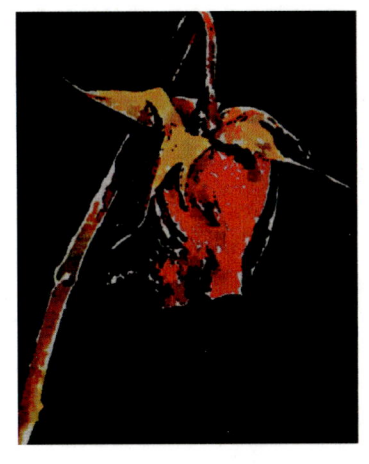

When the children returned home from school their Mother suddenly gasped and stopped the car before driving it into the garage. "My beautiful roses!", she moaned. The roses had been beautifully shades of pink and yellow, plus red and white types just a few days before. Now the flowers were shriveled and their heads were down, stalks bent and the leaves were brown. They also seemed taller, perhaps because they were trying to find the light higher up.

Mother hadn't said anything, but there were fewer types of fruit and vegetables at the supermarket. With no light the farmers had to harvest everything they could, but no new berries, apples, pears, oranges, peaches or other fruit were growing. Vegetables that grow underground, like potatoes and carrots, were being harvested too, but no new ones were growing.

Without sunlight the plant's can't grow and produce seeds or fruit. Mother had bought more canned and frozen fruit and vegetables than usual, but even those were running out.

WEEK 2 - THE TREES START HIBERNATING AND OTHER ODD THINGS

After a few weeks the leaves had dropped off of many trees as they went into the kind of hibernation state that they would be in during a normal winter. Others, such as fir trees, looked very sad because their branches were drooping and their leaves were very pale and dropping off.

The weather became colder every day and the big pond in the park froze over, which Zen and Zelda liked. Father made them some ice skates and hockey sticks. They and their friends played ice hockey. Puzzled ducks and geese waddled around looking for the water, so Zen carefully broke a hole in the ice at the edge of a small pond so that they could feed.

Everybody became very worried about food. Many people, towns and cities had started to try growing food indoors, but it takes time to build indoor farms and for plants to start producing fruit or vegetables.

There had been no rain for several weeks, which was unusual where Zen and Zelda lived. The farmers said that, even if they used artificial lights to give their crops enough light to grow, it wouldn't work without water.

Even worse, with everybody having their lights and heating turned on all the time, electric power companies were struggling to supply enough electricity. Some even had to shut down completely because they relied on special solar panels that turned sunlight into electricity.

The reservoirs, big ponds where water is stored for use in the summer, were emptying and with no rain they might become completely dry. Everybody was told to use as little water as possible. Zen and Zelda really missed their daily shower and Saturday evening bathtime.

THE VANISHING THINGS - OMNIBUS #1

DAY 21 - THE SUN RETURNS

After a few weeks it was all looking very bad and people were miserable and a little bit worried. Then something wonderful happened on Day 21. Zen and Zelda were woken up by strong sunlight coming through their windows and the sounds of birds singing and chattering noisily. They rushed to the window and there it was - their beloved Sun, shining away as normal.

THE EXPLANATION

What had actually happened? Unbeknown to all of the people on Earth, the Sun had decided that it needed a vacation. So, it called a friend somewhere else in our galaxy, and asked them to sit in for three weeks while it went to visit friends.

Unfortunately, the Sun, a young, bright star, had forgotten that their friend was now a dark star. So, there was a dark star at the center of our Solar system, which is why Earth didn't fly off into Outer Space, but it wasn't shining any light on us. "Oops!", said the Sun. "Sorry, Earth, I wasn't thinking."

Thankfully, things returned to normal in just a few days. After four weeks Mother's roses bloomed and looked and smelled beautiful. Everyone rejoiced for a change when it started to rain and the farmers were soon delivering fresh fruit and vegetables to the stores. Life was good again.

It had been a close thing but it all ended well, with everyone on Earth appreciating our Sun much more. Thankfully, the Sun now knows never to go on vacation again without leaving a young star in its place to shine bright, warm rays of sunlight on us. **HooRAY!**

THE END

BOOK #2 - THE VANISHING TREES EPISODE

In which all of the trees suddenly disappear, causing unexpected consequences.

The Vanishing Trees Episode

By Red White

DAY 1 - THE DAY THAT THE TREES STARTED DISAPPEARING

Tommy and Trisha were up early to go to the beach. They put their bathing suits on under some summer clothes and ran out to sit in the car. It was a warm, sunny day without a cloud in the sky. Mum had packed a picnic and Dad had a big bag with a surprise in it. It wasn't far to the beach so they were there in a few minutes. They would normally have walked, but they had extra things to carry today.

As they drove down Sandy Beach Road, they all had a strange feeling that something wasn't quite right, but they were too excited to mention it to each other. Dad parked close to the quiet part of the beach and they unpacked everything, chose a nice spot high on the sand dunes to make their base, and took everything there.

Dad set up the picnic table and chairs and carried everything but the big bag with the surprise in it over from the car so that he and Mum could set everything out for their picnic breakfast. Trisha and Tommy went for a swim in the shallow water. It was a nice beach, with a gently sloping, sandy bottom, so they were quite safe.

There was a headland next to that part of the beach and it had rocky tidepools that were always full of interesting creatures. After their first dip, Trisha said "Let's go and look for crabs and things. Race you there!". They took off at full speed, getting to the biggest pool, which they knew well, at exactly the same time. Trisha was a year older than Tommy, but he was as fast a runner as her.

They found some hermit crabs with their shell homes on their backs, and lots of small fishes. They also found, but didn't disturb, some seahorses hiding amongst a frondy seaweed plant. It was good to see them there, because Mum had told them that the seahorses could only live in very clean water.

They also saw a strange creature, unlike

anything they'd seen before. It was shaped like a beetle but with scales, like an armadillo. It was only a few inches long, with multicolored markings. It moved very slowly, settling on a fine seaweed patch attached to a rock. Dad said that it was a Lined Chiton and went over to look at it for himself.

The picnic breakfast was perfect, with croissants, cheese, cold meat, pickles, tomatoes, apples, oranges, chocolate muffins and homemade ginger beer. Tommy and Trisha tidied up after they had finished eating while Dad unzipped the bag with the surprise in it. He pulled out some sections of rod and some zippered bags with something flat inside of them. He screwed the short rods together then screwed one end of the assembly into a heavy metal disk. He made two of them.

Tommy helped him carry them onto a flat part of the beach. Then he strung a net between the rods and they realized that he had built a badminton net. Sure enough, out came the racquets and a shuttlecock. Dad drew lines in the sand to mark the court of play.

They started with Mum and Tommy playing against Dad and Trisha, then Dad and Tommy against Mum and Trisha. Mum and Dad went back to the picnic spot to pack things up while Tommy and Trisha played against each other until it was time to go home.

It wasn't until they arrived home and drove towards the garage that Dad suddenly exclaimed "The trees have gone! All of them - vanished!". They jumped out of the car and ran into the backyard, expecting to see the trees fallen on the ground, but they weren't there. The only signs that they had ever grown in the yard were some bare patches of earth. Oddly, the flowers, plants and shrubs were all there, along with the grassy lawn.

"That's very strange.", said Dad. "The trees over on the headland by the tide pools were still there and I think that I saw the small wood on the edge of town." Mum agreed - "Yes", they looked fine. Maybe they are a different type of tree to the ones that we had." Dad was quite annoyed that his apple, orange and lemon trees were gone. He was very proud of them and everyone enjoyed the fruit from them. In fact, they had just eaten the last of the oranges for breakfast. They went indoors, feeling puzzled and a litte sad. The children finished their homework while Mum and Dad quietly debated what might have happened.

DAY 2 - PEOPLE NOTICE MANY MORE TREES VANISHING

Dad dropped Tommy and Trisha off at school on his way to work. Almost everywhere they looked, the trees were gone. The big oak tree outside the school entrance had left a really large brown patch of soil behind, just like the missing ones in their backyard. Everyone had run into the playground to see if the wood at the other side of it was still there. It was, but there were far fewer trees.

Tommy's teacher greeted the class and said that they were going to watch a short program on the Serious Education Channel along with the other classes, so they went to the main hall, which had a very large TV screen. Trisha was already there and she waved to Tommy as he came in. They had both guessed what the program must be about.

The program started with an aerial view of the town. The narrator pointed out the brown patches in peoples' yards and in the parks around town. The problem was widespread. The scene changed to a serious looking interviewer introducing an even more serious looking scientist. He was introduced as being a dendrologist - an expert on trees.

"We've all noticed that a lot of trees have vanished", said the interviewer. "Professor, can you explain what has happened? Have you ever seen anything like this before?". The Professor paused for a second, then answered "No, this is unlike anything that I, or anybody that I know, have ever encountered before. It started overnight and we first heard reports yesterday morning. It appears to be happening all over the world. Individual trees simply disappear. About one in four trees in woods and forests have disappeared, but we expect more of them may disappear, so we're keeping a continual watch on them wherever we can."

The Professor went on to explain that it isn't unusual for trees to die gradually because of known pests or diseases. Dutch Elm Disease caused many countries in Europe to lose most of their Dutch Elm trees many years ago, but the cause was traced to a fungus spread by beetles that burrow into the tree bark. The disease was eventually halted by controlling the beetles and vaccinating important trees.

The children returned to their regular classes, but it was hard to concentrate when such a strange thing had happened. Children were passing notes around when their teacher wasn't looking, mostly containing some quite funny explanations for what had happened to the trees, such as "It was the Buzzsaw Goblin", or "The woodpeckers ate them all." Or "Aliens collected them for fuel for their spaceship". Unfortunately, none of them made any sense, or were even close to the truth.

DAY 3 - NO MORE TREES

The day started as normal, but when the children arrived at school they found that all of the trees in the woods at the other side of the playground had gone. They asked their teacher if she had heard of other woods disappearing. She looked a bit sad and said, "Yes, they were reporting on the news this morning that the huge Redwood and Douglas Fir forests have disappeared. So have all of the trees in the Amazon rainforest."

Lessons proceeded as normal for the rest of the day, but everybody was a little quieter than usual. Nobody joked or played tricks. People tried to focus on their schoolwork, though there was a lot more speculation at break and lunch times. Imaginations ran amok, with crazy ideas like aliens stealing the trees for their own planet, a new bacteria that could digest trees in an instant and gnomes that could magically make things vanish at will. The most popular theory was that the trees had become infected with something that made them burst, just like a bubble that has gotten too big.

At this point, there was very little discussion about the impact of the trees having disappeared. Trees are just trees, right? Maybe they would start growing again, or scientists could modify other plants or shrubs to grow like trees. Nobody had been to the forests where the Redwoods had been, or the Amazon rainforest, so it was hard to imagine what they had been like, or what they might look like now.

The birds and squirrels were much more concerned though. They had lost their homes overnight, ending up on the ground or flying to buildings to roost. People reported seeing huge flocks of birds flying South, looking for new places to live, preferably with lots of trees.

The squirrels were living in bushes and started nesting on people's houses. Some even got into the school and had to be removed by the janitor. The teachers decided that the school should build a nesting box for the squirrels so that they would be safe at night.

WEEK 1 - SHOPS START RUNNING SHORT OF GOODS

Mother came home from the store looking a bit bothered. There were no fresh oranges and apples and pears were hard to find. The storekeeper told her that they were expecting supplies of some things, like bananas and avocados, as those were in transit in refrigerated ships, trains or trucks, but they would run out soon too. She had to buy frozen fruit instead, but wondered how long supplies of those would last before they were all gone.

The stores had already run out of paper goods, like kitchen towels, toilet paper and facial tissues. Paper is produced from the wood from trees. Newspaper and magazine publishers reduced the number of pages and the size of the pages to save paper, as it was running out. Most had online versions of their publications, but it would soon be a big problem for printers.

Everything from books to posters and labels on jars and cans would have to be printed on plastic instead of paper. New plastics would be needed to replace the paper used in computer printers that were used for everything from letters to office documents. Cardboard boxes, paper shopping bags and wrapping paper would need to be replaced by plastic products too.

WEEK 2 - REAL SHORTAGES

It had been two weeks since the trees had all vanished. There were no nuts, bananas, apples, pears, oranges or avocados in the stores and it was hard to find even frozen fruit, other than berries. Tommy and Trisha were horrified to discover that there was no more chocolate and that their breakfast waffles came with berries and cream but no maple syrup. All of the missing food items had come from trees.

Mother was upset because some spices that she used whilst baking, such as nutmeg, cloves and cinnamon, were no longer available. Dad was upset because there was no coffee. He ran out just before the last few coffee filters were used up. They were made of paper, which came from the wood from trees. He would have switched to making his coffee in a percolator, but that wasn't possible now. He switched to drinking tea instead.

The new houses being built near the school were half finished when the wooden lumber used to build them ran out. Trisha's friend told her that her Aunt and Uncle had been waiting for one of them to be finished so that they could move in. The builder said that they were looking into using metal instead of wood, but it was already in short supply and more expensive than wood. They would have to use metal or plastic doors instead of the elegant wooden ones that they had chosen and the matching cabinets would now be made from metal and painted to look like wooden ones.

He didn't know when he would be able to get the replacements, so he was making plans to get the roof finished with artificial tiles before the winter came. At least they would have somewhere to live, but it might be a while before everything was finished.

WEEK 4 - THE WEATHER CHANGES

The builder had just finished putting the roofs on the new houses when it suddenly started to rain every day. People living on the hills were in danger, as, with no trees to suck up the water, flash floods and mudslides were becoming a huge problem. Many houses had to be abandoned because they had slipped downhill and become too dangerous to live in. Some even floated off downstream.

Similar problems were being reported worldwide. The debris from damaged buildings was causing havoc in reservoirs, threatening to damage dams, and in ports, where it was a hazard to ships. People returning from cruises told stories of seeing whole houses floating around in the ocean. Some resourceful people had taken to trying to salvage the wood from them and selling it. In poor countries it was being sold as firewood.

Scientists reported that the amount of oxygen in the air was decreasing alarmingly, with more carbon dioxide gas being present. Trees and plants convert carbon dioxide to oxygen, helping animals stay alive, as we all depend on it to breathe. The weather reports warned of large increases in temperatures, making wildfires more likely and changing the climate so much that some crops would no longer grow. They were afraid that droughts could cause people to have to abandon some cities altogether as there would be no water for them.

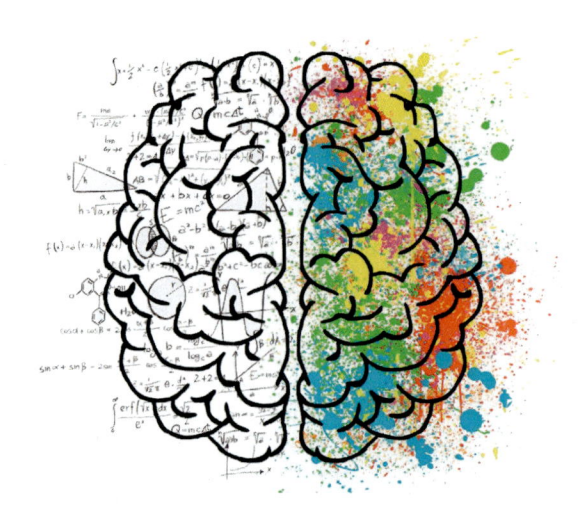

Scientists everywhere worked hard to figure out how to cope with the problem. The government was drawing up plans to help farmers move to areas that were more suited to the crops that were needed. In some cases that even meant moving to neighboring countries. The situation was getting worse and there were no solutions in sight.

MONTH 2 - SOMETHING WONDERFUL HAPPENS

Mother was usually the first person up in the morning as she prepared breakfast for everyone, though Dad generally did that on Sundays. It was dark as she put the kettle on and laid the table for breakfast. Dad and the children had just come downstairs when Mum opened the blinds to let some early morning sunlight in.

She gasped and turned around suddenly, pointing out of the window. "The trees, the trees, they're all back!", she cried. Everyone ran outside. Dad was so happy to see his fruit trees that he ran around hugging each one in turn and saying how glad he was to see them again.

None of the trees looked at all damaged, though there was no fruit on them. They were all a little smaller than they had been before they vanished, but not by much. They certainly looked healthy. As it was the weekend Dad suggested that they take a quick drive around town to check out the other trees.
Sure enough, not only were the trees back in people's yards, the wood near the school and the trees on the headland by the beach were all back too. Soon they would be filled with bird nests and the squirrels would move back in. They really hadn't liked being so close to the humans and their pets, especially the dogs that chased them.

Within a week or two the weather started to get back to normal and grocery stores were starting to take pre-orders for some kinds of fruit. Soon after that the builder was able to resume work on the new houses. It took a few months for fruit and paper goods to start reappearing in the stores, but most people acted sensibly and didn't buy more than they really needed .

THE EXPLANATION

It took a while for the scientists to figure out what had happened. What they had failed to notice at first was that the areas where there had been trees were hiding something. After a couple of months, little saplings started to appear and there was a hope that the trees would eventually grow back, but it would take many years.

However, when they did come back, they all reappeared overnight and were about the same size that they had originally been. It was a big puzzle. How could they vanish then reappear like that? It took a while for pieces of the puzzle to come together, starting with a discovery that the Earth had passed through a mysterious electromagnetic region. Astronomers thought that it had probably resulted from a tiny piece of the Sun's material breaking off and being thrown out into space.

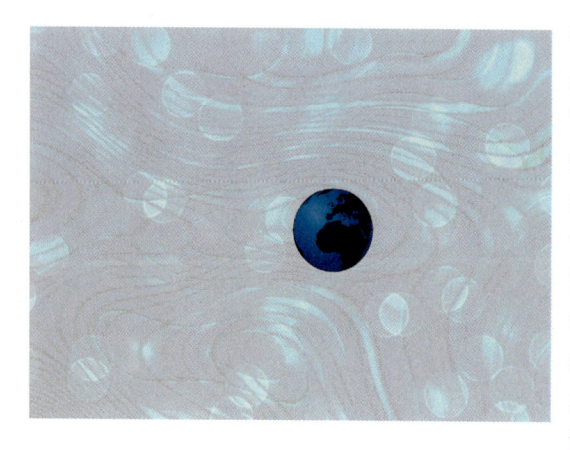

That happens quite often, with the events being known as solar flares. They can interfere with radio communications, sometimes even damaging satellites beyond repair. The scientists who track such things took no notice of it until an astronomer pointed out that the direction that the electromagnetic energy had come from was from a point outside of our solar system, not from the Sun.

He also noted that the Earth had moved into the strange region the day that the trees started disappearing and out of it the day before they all reappeared. It had to be more than a coincidence, but how could it be involved?

The answer was astonishing. A botanist pointed out the fact that some plants appear to respond to threats by producing substances that signal the danger to other plants, so that they can try to protect themselves. They can't, of course, just run away, but they can make themselves less attractive to predators, such as beetles or insects, usually by emitting some kind of chemical.

We will probably never know exactly what happened, but the best theory to date is that the trees simply melted into the ground and left behind some kind of seed that preserved enough information to allow them to reconstruct themselves after the danger was gone. They did find some strange substances in the soil near the trees and are still analyzing it.

All that they know so far is that putting any kind of tree seed in a solution of water with it results in almost instantaneous growth of the tree. That discovery alone was worthwhile, but scientists haven't yet worked out how to make more of the amazing substance. Maybe, one day, they will, and we'll all be able to grow any kind of tree that we like. The kids' Dad would like that!

THE END

Acknowledgement

The excellent image of the Lined Chiton was created by Kirt L. Onthank and was distributed under the Creative Commons Attribution-Share Alike 3.0 Unported license which can be viewed at https://creativecommons.org/licenses/by-sa/3.0/legalcode.

BOOK 3 - THE VANISHING BATTERIES AFFAIR

The day that all of the batteries in the World disappeared and what happened next.

The Vanishing Batteries Affair

By Red White

DAY 1 - MYSTERIOUS DISAPPEARANCES

Beryl and Barry had just finished setting up the miniature train set that Barry had received as a birthday present. It was unusual in that the train was pulled by a battery powered locomotive. The track was basically a loop with two sets of points that allowed the train to change direction. There was a tunnel and a station. A remote control allowed Barry to start, stop and control the speed of the train. Mother called them for their afternoon snack, so Barry switched the train and its controller off to save battery power.

After they'd eaten, Barry returned to his new toy. He switched the locomotive on, then the controller. He was puzzled when the controller didn't light up to allow him to control the train. He shook it, then opened the battery compartment to make sure that they were securely installed. It was empty! Out of curiosity, he uncoupled the locomotive, turned it over and opened its battery compartment. It was empty too!

Barry ran to find Beryl, as he was sure that she was playing tricks on him. Beryl was adamant that it wasn't her. "You came to the table after me and left it before me", said Beryl. "I can't have done it. Mother was here the whole time too. It's a mystery", she declared. "Never mind", said Mother. "There are more batteries in the storage cupboard. Father bought a lot of them last weekend." Barry ran to the cupboard but came back looking very puzzled. "There aren't any batteries in there", he said. "Neither the ones that I need nor the ones that we use in other things."

"Don't worry", said Mother. "I'll be going to the store at three o'clock and I'll buy some more. Maybe Father had to use them all for something". She looked at the clock on the wall then checked her watch. Both had stopped just ten minutes ago, at the same time. She took the clock off of the wall to check its batteries. They were gone!

A few hours later, father called to say that he would be late home as his car wouldn't start, so he would take the light rail train and walk the rest of the way. He'd sort the car issue out the next day, Saturday. He also said that he'd tried calling Mother's cellphone first, but it had gone straight to voicemail. Mother checked it, only to find that the battery was dead. She plugged it in to recharge it, but nothing happened. She sighed and decided to wait until Father arrived.

DAY 2 - THEORIES START TO EMERGE

When Beryl and Barry arrived at school the next morning they were told to go to the main hall after stashing their coats and belongings. The Principal was there, talking with a few of the teachers. One of them was tuning the TV into the Serious Education Channel for a special news item covering the battery disappearances.

The program started with a serious looking announcer outlining the problem. She then turned to a serious looking man who was introduced as an Electrochemical Engineer. He specialized in improving battery technologies and developing new kinds of batteries. The announcer asked him if this was a problem that could be fixed quickly by simply building new batteries. "He immediately replied "Unfortunately, not. We've tried that, of course, but when we mix the chemicals that go into a battery they seem OK but after the batteries are made they disappear within twenty four hours. We can't explain it yet."

He went on to say "It doesn't appear to be a purely chemical issue, because we can't detect any new chemicals after the disappearance of a newly mixed substance. We did notice a temporary energy surge in the vicinity though, making us think that this is a physical and not a chemical process."

Barry put his hand up to ask a question. "Yes, young man?", said the engineer. "Are there any other chemicals that could be used to make batteries?", asked Barry. "I'm glad you asked that", said the engineer. "We've been looking at lots of alternatives for a long time, but it will take a while to work out how to manufacture millions of new batteries quickly, but we'll do the best that we can. We're not the only people working on the problem."

With that they all returned to their regular classes, but lots of notes were circulated with some quite good and many hilariously silly ideas about why the batteries had disappeared. They included:
- The batteries had instantaneously moved into another dimension, or an alternative universe that we can't see.
- The engine makers stole them all to stop people buying electric cars.
- They'd all gone on vacation and would be back soon.
- A mysterious energy surge had made them vaporize.

RED WHITE

- Magical gnomes had made them disappear.
- The bunnies ate them all.

DAY 3 - WIDESPREAD REPORTS OF BATTERY DISAPPEARANCES

Dad's car wasn't the only one to have stopped working. All gas and diesel powered cars rely on batteries to start the engine. Only very old gas powered engines can be started by hand. Electric vehicles were completely useless because they depend on large and powerful batteries to drive their motors.

Some trains that used overhead electrical cables or a third "live" rail were still running, but the crucial ones needed for hauling goods around the country had diesel engines, so they were stuck wherever they happened to be when it was time to start the engine.

Most commercial aircraft were grounded too. Although many small planes can be started by swinging the propeller to get the engine started and commercial jets need a jump start from a generator, all of the electronic systems needed to fly the plane and run equipment on board have a battery backup in case the main generator fails. Of course, you have to get the generator started first and that would probably require a battery. The government had quickly decided that they couldn't risk allowing planes to fly without a backup power system in place, which would mean installing some kind of self-starting generator.

Shipping was affected less because modern ships have standby generators that provide energy to power lighting and essential controls if the main generator fails.

39

It wasn't just the children's toys that stopped working when the batteries disappeared. Almost all of their toys, apart from balls and old board games, needed batteries. Their cellphones, tablet computers and Dad's laptop computer all needed batteries. Without the battery in place they still couldn't use some of those devices even when they were plugged into the electricity supply.

Besides most of the clocks, other household items stopped working too, ranging from flashlights and emergency lights to handy kitchen gadgets and power tools. The full extent of the problem was only just becoming clear.

WEEK 1 - SERIOUS SHORTAGES

Unlike most other times when things were in short supply, people couldn't hoard batteries as there weren't any and none were being made. So, attention shifted to alternatives, such as solar panels, that produce electricity from the sun, and small generators. The shops quickly ran short of both and people were warned that it could take months for manufacturers to be able to deliver new ones to stores because no trains, trucks or delivery vans were working.

Because most goods that we buy in a store aren't made locally, the manufacturers and shopkeepers had to come up with ways to deliver things without vehicles that need batteries. The railway companies were busy buying generators or devices that would allow them to use mains electricity to start locomotives. Once started they would be kept running until a new jumpstarting site was reached. Cargo ships were being fitted with auxiliary sails so that they wouldn't have to completely rely on their engines.

At the more local level, people started using horses and carts to deliver things and horse drawn water barges or sailing ships to move things along waterways. That was what had happened for hundreds, or even thousands, of years before the mechanized age. Even so, the effect on supplies of everyday goods was completely disrupted. Many stores had almost completely empty shelves.

Even the flow of news about the situation was being disrupted. Almost all TV cameras have batteries, so the broadcasters were going back to cameras driven by a generator, which is exactly what they'd used in the early days of what was then known as "outside broadcasting", and which we now call "live coverage". Thankfully, for those who could power a phone, tablet or computer from the mains electricity supply, the Internet was still functional, as the critical equipment used to transport information across it all had standby power sources.

Perhaps the worst effects were in areas where medical supplies were running short. Governments across the world were doing everything that they could to move medicines and equipment to the places where they were most needed. Some extraordinary efforts were made to get supplies to areas that desperately needed them. One that caught the headlines was a hundred mile long "human chain" formed by people handing supplies from one to another, all along the chain. It was slow and tiring, but effective.

WEEK 2 - THE PLOT THICKENS

The children were all tired of walking to school, so they were allowed to ride their bikes. As it was actually shorter to cut across the park than having to drive around it, Beryl and Barry could leave home five minutes later, which they liked. It was cold hanging around in the playground waiting to be allowed into school.

After they had stashed their belongings they went to the main hall for another broadcast from the Serious Education Channel. The same serious looking announcer was there again, along with the serious looking Electrochemical Engineer whom she had interviewed in the early days of the vanishing battery episode. There was also a serious looking lady who was introduced as a Detective Chief Inspector.

"Viewers, we have an update on the vanished batteries. First, an explanation from our expert." He stepped forward to the microphone, coughed to clear his throat, and started his explanation. "After a lot of research, we have discovered exactly what happened to the batteries", he said. Somebody mixed a previously unknown substance in with the metals used to make batteries. Not the chemicals inside, but the battery casing itself.

This can't have been an accident on such a wide scale, so we decided to ask the detectives and researchers at the County's police forensics unit for help. Over to the Detective Chief Inspector…"

She stepped to the microphone and smiled, which was highly unusual on the Serious Education Channel, causing the announcer to raise her eyebrows in shock before she regained her composure. "Having discovered the fact that the problem was probably due to something that affected the metals in the battery casings, we went to the manufacturer of the metal to see if they had any on stock that hadn't been used to make the batteries that disappeared. Thankfully, there are only a handful of very large manufacturers who make that particular metal and we found one that had samples that were of interest to us."

The Electromechanical Engineer held up a small sheet of what looked like regular aluminum for everyone to see. "It looks completely normal," said the Detective Chief Inspector, "but our scientists found that it contains two types of material that combine when a powerful radio pulse is broadcast. That's when something very strange happens…" The engineer took up the story. "When these two substances combine they immediately vaporize the aluminum casing and start an electrochemical reaction that causes the battery chemicals to turn into a mixture of harmless gasses. The battery simply disappears!"

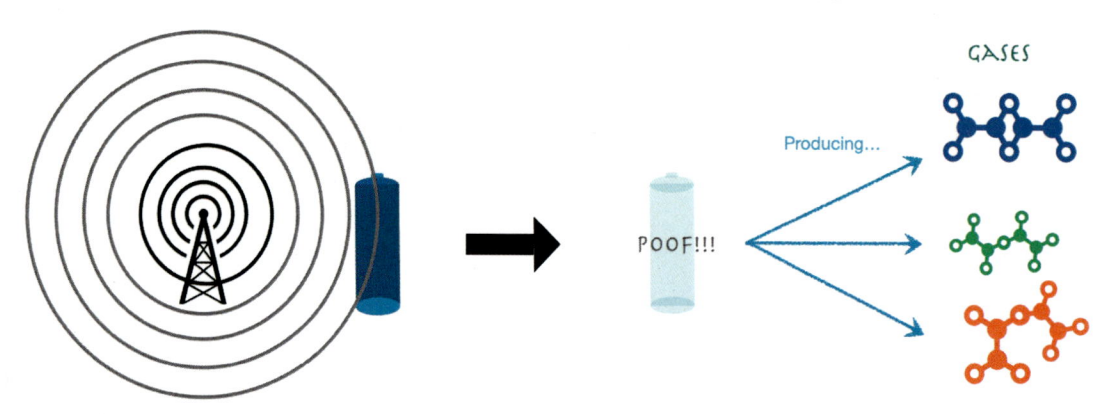

"We are searching for the culprits", said the Detective Chief Inspector, "and hope to find and apprehend them soon. Meanwhile, the battery manufacturers have restarted their production lines and batteries will start being sent out to transportation companies and health facilities in the next few days."

The serious looking announcer wrapped things up by promising to broadcast the complete information once the Police had finished their work. The children returned to their normal curriculum feeling much happier. By the time they arrived home Mother had heard the news and Father was obviously relieved when he came in. He had a long bicycle ride to and from his office. "Great news!", he said. "Things should all return to normal soon". They all slept very well that night.

MONTH 1 - ALL IS EXPLAINED

Father arrived home early and excited. "Quick! Turn the evening news on, please.", he said. Mother changed from the Gentle Meditation Channel to the Urgent News Channel. She was just in time. An ugent looking journalist had just started his update on the vanishing batteries story.

"The Federal Investigation Organization announced minutes ago that they had tracked down the perpetrators of this terrible affair with the help of the International Police Organization and arrested a gang of 24 villains hiding out on MacPenguin Island, halfway between New Zealand and Antarctica. It is so remote that they had to ask for the help of the Navy to take them there and land them in Cold Cove at the South of the island by helicopter. Usually, the only inhabitants in that area are penguins. The nearest humans are at a scientific research station at the Northern tip of the island."

He continued - "The gang was found in a large cave that they had adapted for their purposes. Scientific research satellites had pinpointed the site of the radio burst that triggered the reactions that caused the batteries to vaporize, but there was no sign of a radio station. So, the nearest Coastguard services sent a reconnaissance plane out to look for any signs of the gang and were lucky enough to spot them preparing a mobile telescoping radio mast that they had just moved out of the cave to rebroadcast the radio signal and destroy newly made batteries. We also found a laboratory with strange apparatus that we are trying to understand. They haven't admitted what they were plotting next, but the important thing is that they are all behind bars awaiting trial."

"What we know so far is that the group had been put together by a rogue amateur scientist who claimed to have invented a whole new energy source that would put battery makers out of business. He had secretly approached many manufacturing companies to fund the completion of his research, but he couldn't prove his claims and none of them wanted to become involved with what looked like an expensive waste of money.

At that point he decided to force the World to look at his claims by hatching his dastardly plot. He was a skilled chemist and he stumbled upon a combination of two substances that would achieve his aim. The actual substances are being kept secret, for obvious reasons. He couldn't risk setting up a radio station where it would arouse suspicions, so he researched remote, but reachable, islands and chose Macquarie Island.

The most difficult part of his plot was planting the substances in the battery casing materials. He did that by convincing the metal manufacturers that they could make a lighter, stronger casing by including his specially formulated additive. That would save them metal and increase their profits, so it was an easy sell. Little did they know that they were enabling a fiendish plot.

The rest, as we say, is history. His invention did make the batteries disappear, but the nature of the substance was discovered much more quickly than he had anticipated. Like most villains, he had overlooked a crucial possibility and had to postpone the announcement of his claimed invention as it would draw unwanted attention. He had been hoping for things to become more dire before approaching some of the companies that had turned him down previously. Instead, he and his cronies are safely locked up. Now it's back to the studio for the urgent sports news."

The whole family rejoiced. Father had pre-ordered a car battery and he had just heard that he could pick it up tomorrow, so he promised that the family would go for a picnic down by the beach to celebrate. Mother decided to bake a cake, which she was very good at. Her cakes were always delicious and nourishing. The children were happy that they would soon be able to use their toys again. Barry decided to bring his train set out in preparation and Beryl went off to find her memory testing game as she had temporarily forgotten where it was. All would soon be back to normal. The terrible affair of the vanishing batteries was drawing to a close.

THE END

BOOK #4 - THE VANISHING INSECTS OCCURRENCE

In which all of the insects disappear, what happened and the extraordinary reason.

The Vanishing Insects Occurrence

By Red White

DAY 1 - THE SILENT CHANGE

Irina and Ian had just returned from a Saturday morning shopping trip with their parents. They ran outside to check Rosie and Robby, their pet rabbits. They were contentedly chewing away at a nice fresh patch of weeds that had popped up at the edge of Dad's prize lawn. Ian went to check the water in their hutch and decided to change it, so he took the bowl indoors, washed it and brought out a fresh bowl full of cold water.

As he came out of the door he stopped and looked up at the telephone line that ran from a pole at the back of the garden to the eaves of their house. There were dozens of birds sitting on it and the cable that supported it. That was very odd, as they were swifts and he'd never seen that many sitting still for more than a few seconds. They were always flying around catching insects wherever they could find them. He pointed them out to Irina, who also thought it very odd.

After lunch they drove to the local farm for some organic produce. The farmer didn't use any chemicals on his crops and they were fresh off of the field or trees, so they were healthier to eat than the ones bought in a store. When they arrived the farmer's wife gave them each an apple. She also gave the children small bags of food. Irina and Ian ran over to the duck pond to feed the ducks. They swam towards the children, quacking noisily.

When all of the food was gone they ran over to the bee hives to talk to the farmer, who was also a beekeeper. He had just closed one of the hives and was taking his hat off. It had a veil to keep any angry bees away from his face, though he told them that he had only ever been stung when he touched a bee accidentally. Today he was looking perplexed though.

"All of my bees have gone", he said. There had been no signs that they were about to swarm, and even then, they always came back to their hives. "I must phone around the other farms and beekeepers to see if they have been spotted anywhere", he said, hurrying towards the farmhouse. Father said that it was time to go home as they had bought everything that they needed, so they climbed in the car and drove home. "Don't worry", he said. I'm sure that the bees will come back before dusk.

DAY 3 - PEOPLE BECOME CONCERNED

Nobody mentioned the missing bees again until Monday. Just before lunch, pupils were told to go to the school hall for a special news broadcast. Irina's teacher was tuning in to the Serious Education Channel. The children were surprised to see their friend the beekeeper standing in front of his empty hives and saying that they had now been gone for over two days and that all of the neighboring beekeepers were reporting the same thing. "We don't believe that this is the result of bee kidnapping", he said. "Thieves always take the hives, honeycombs and bees, not just the bees. It's hard to get them to abandon their eggs and honey. We're appealing to the public to immediately let us know if they see swarms of bees anywhere. We've set up a free hotline. Just call 1-800-BZZZZZZ."

The program returned to the studio, where the serious looking announcer said "So, there have been widespread reports of bees going missing. It started on Saturday and doesn't appear to only be a local problem. We are hearing similar reports from across the country. No dead bees have been found, so it is a mystery. Let's see what our expert has to say." She introduced a serious looking lady who was an entomologist, a scientist who studies insects.

"What do you think has happened?", asked the announcer. The entomologist looked a little worried and said "We're not sure. We have been studying the disappearance of bees for many years. However, those disappearances generally result in the death of some or all of the bees in a hive. They don't just vanish. We have many theories about what is happening, mainly focused on accidental poisoning because of substances used to grow or treat crops close to bee habitats. This map shows the most affected areas."

"Could they have been stolen?", asked the announcer. "That's unlikely", said the entomologist, "The beekeeper was right. Thieves always take the hives and contents, not just the bees. My colleagues reported that the bees and ladybugs that we have in our lab to study their habits and health have also disappeared, further deepening the mystery. The only ones that are left are dead ones that we found whilst researching the recent mysterious increase in bee deaths." The announcer thanked her and promised that they would track the story as it evolved.

WEEK 1. HONEY SHORTAGES

It was Saturday and time to go shopping, so they took the car into town. They noticed that a lot of shelves in the produce section were empty, mostly the nuts and berries, but also some seasonal fruit. As they drove past a row of stores Father pointed out all of the birds sitting on the roofs, looking a little forlorn. Then he surprised them by pulling into their favorite diner. "Let's treat ourselves to lunch today", he said. "We can eat outside if there's a table", said Mother. It's warm enough and we need some sun.

They each chose a dish, Father ordered some appetizers to share and Mother ordered a selection of fruit and cheeses for dessert. They were tucking into dessert, which was laid out on three large platters, when there was a sudden flurry of wings and several dozen starlings descended on the table and started stealing the fruit! They had to abandon their meal as it was now spoiled. "That is really strange", said Mother. Maybe it's because they don't have any insects to feed on."

Mother suggested that they go to the farm on the way home to see if they had any fruit. They also had really nice butter, eggs and freshly baked bread, which would go well with Sunday's breakfast. As usual, the children took some food over to the ducks while their parents shopped. The only problem was that the farmer's wife didn't have any honey. "We only ever collect and bottle enough for a few days", she said, "and the honey left in the hives was soon gone. The bees haven't returned and the beekeepers are all very worried about the situation."

55

She went on to describe how they had lost a lot of near-ripe fruit to the birds. They didn't usually damage much of the fruit, as they liked it to be nice and ripe, but were obviously hungry. "The real problem is that it will be difficult to pollinate the flowers on the trees next season", said the farmer's wife. "The bees usually do that for us. We're talking with experts at the local Agricultural College to work out the easiest and most effective way to handle the problem".

MONTH 1 - WIDESPREAD PROBLEMS

The insects had been gone for a month, resulting in shortages of all kinds of fruit, nuts and honey. Even produce such as cucumbers, melons, tomatoes, peppers and green beans was very hard to find. Mother had to modify a lot of the family's favorite recipes by substituting other things wherever she could.

Everybody had become used to the birds foraging in bins and a lot of people were putting scraps of food out for them. Ian's friend said that he had seen an armadillo rummaging through their bin for food, having tipped it over. Armadillos usually feed on grubs, beetles and other insects. Although they also eat plants and other things, this one obviously had a taste for insects.

The only positive things that people were saying about the missing insects came from sportsmen, campers and hikers, whio were happy to not be pursued by mosquitoes and other pests. Farmers had reported seeing absolutely no insects of any kind for weeks, so the ones who used chemicals to protect their crops were happy to save money, but only if they could actually grow the crops that they usually depended upon.

There were some other unexpected consequences too. The Department of Defense put out an urgent request for any silk that people could spare. The parachute manufacturers had run out of it and weren't happy with the other materials that they had tried substituting. Silk is extremely light and strong, making it an ideal parachute cloth.

MONTH 2 - THE INSECTS RETURN

It happened as quietly as it had begun. Irina and Ian arrived at school to find most of the children gathered around something at the edge of a playground. They ran over to see what was going on. One of the children turned around and signaled them to slow down and proceed quietly. They peered over the shoulders of the other children, most of them down on one knee, looking at the bushes. There were two butterflies on the flowers! How could that be?

Just before lunch, the teachers went with the pupils to the large hall. The TV was already tuned into the Serious Education Channel, which was showing a clip of its upcoming series on "Why We Should Eat More Seaweed - A Four Episode Series". The program that they were all awaiting started with a serious looking announcer introducing the serious entomologist who had explained the situation at the start of the vanishing insects occurrence. She went on to ask "What's happened and can you explain it?".

The entomologist answered enthusiastically "The insects have returned, all over the World, which is great news, of course. Bees are back in their hives, or collecting nectar and spreading pollen between plants. The birds and animals that depend on insects for a substantial part of their diet are moving back to their normal habitats, which will make people, especially farmers, very happy." She turned to the screen behind her, which was showing a cross section of the Earth and its atmosphere.

One of the more controversial theories about the disappearance of the insects was that some subtle change in our atmosphere had caused them all to move to much higher altitudes where the oxygen is thinner but there may be other gasses or airborne particles that they depend upon. The children thought that she was about to elaborate on that theory. Instead, she started by saying "We've ruled out all theories about the insects moving to higher altitudes, unknown latitudes or underwater. The reasons are complicated but we needn't worry about them now. Sometimes scientists, like people in any other endeavor, get lucky. Two months ago there was a slight change in something that our sensors, both ground and satellite based, were monitoring. It was a change in the densities of some of the layers that make up the Earth." She pointed at the diagram, then stopped for a few seconds to sip a glass of water.

She continued - "We and all living plants and creatures live in the sea, on the surface of the Earth or in the lowest levels of the atmosphere. We believe that the Earth has four distinct spherical layers: the upper mantle, which we think of as the ground; the lower mantle, which is very hot and dense, but which occasionally breaks through the upper mantle as lava flows from volcanoes; the outer core, which is made of liquid iron and nickel and generates the Earth's magnetic field; and the inner core, which is solid metal, mostly iron and nickel. Oddly, it rotates slightly faster than the outer layers."

INNER CORE

UNKNOWN ZONE

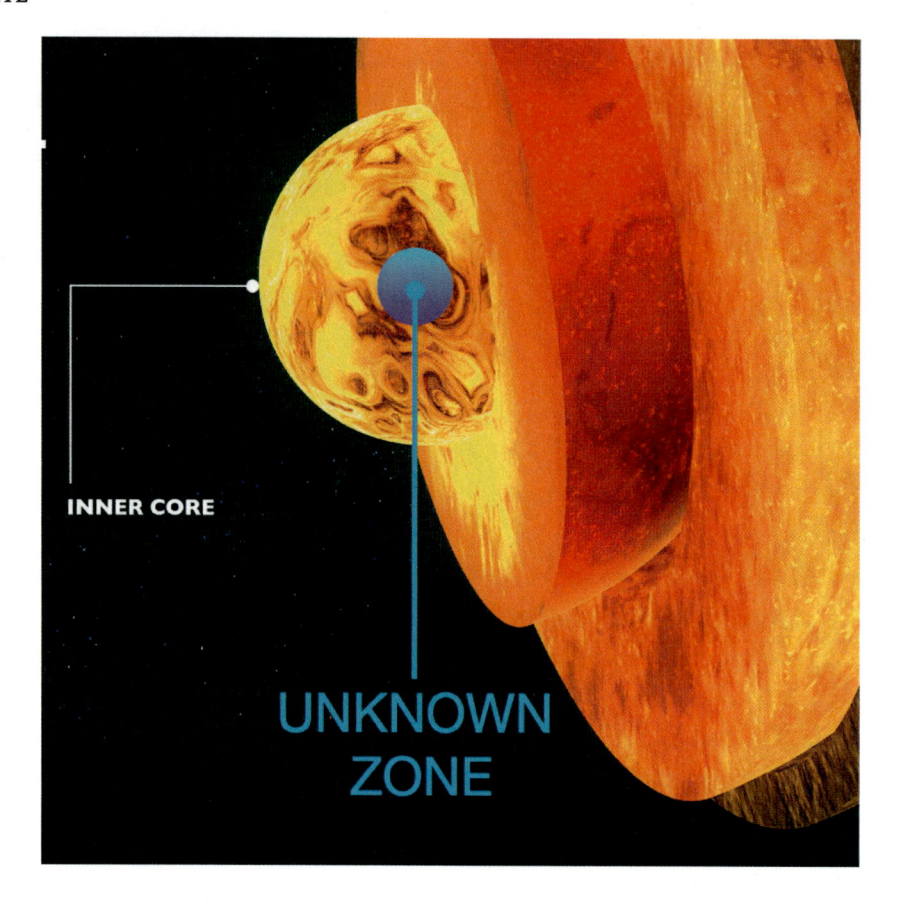

"I think that I understand," said the announcer, "but how does that relate to the insects and their vanishing act?" The entomologist carried on "I'm sorry, I digress a little. I'm not a geologist, but that minor change in the density of the inner core was very puzzling to them. Density is the mass of an object divided by its volume. The higher the density the heavier things of the same size will feel. The change was really, really small, about one billionth of the normal mass of the inner core. They thought that it might have been the result of some material being transferred from the outer core to the inner core. Another theory was that a really dense small innermost "Unknown Zone" had formed."

The next few sentences had everyone on the edges of their seats. "Quite by accident, a colleague of mine noticed that the increase in weight was almost exactly what our estimates of the weight of all of the insects on Earth might be, around 1 billion tons. It didn't seem likely that there was a connection though, until the geologists noticed that there was a quite rapid change going on. First, the inner core got lighter and the outer core got heavier. Then the inner mantle got heavier and the outer core got lighter. Finally, just a few days ago, the outer mantle got heavier and the inner mantle got lighter."

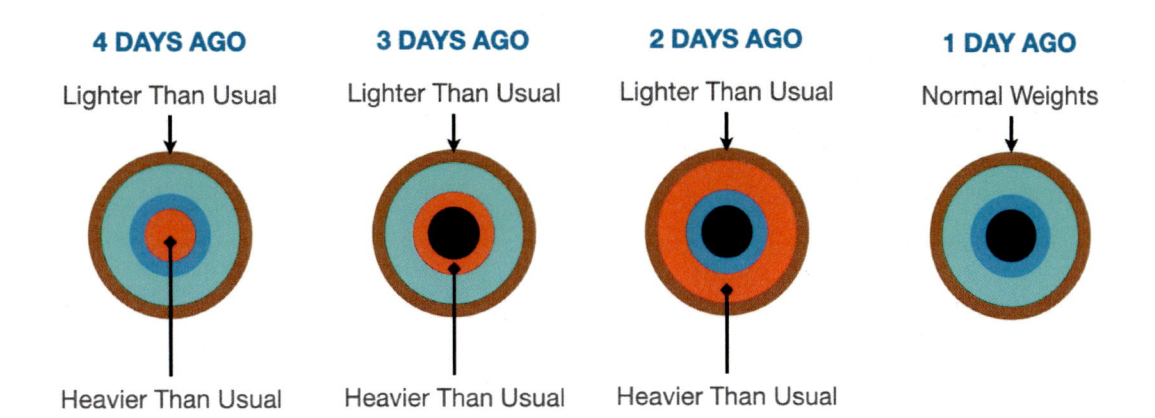

4 DAYS AGO	3 DAYS AGO	2 DAYS AGO	1 DAY AGO
Lighter Than Usual	Lighter Than Usual	Lighter Than Usual	Normal Weights
Heavier Than Usual	Heavier Than Usual	Heavier Than Usual	

Irina couldn't help herself any more "Something was moving from the inner core back to the surface!", she exclaimed. The teacher paused the TV and said "That's an interesting theory, Irina. Now let's hear the rest of the explanation." She unpaused the program. "The entomologists worked with the geologists to see if we could detect anything that might indicate underground movements of the insects.", said the entomologist. Just yesterday we found evidence of traces of compounds that could only come from insects deep inside or below caves around the globe.

Over the previous twenty four hours, insects have poured out of those caves and returned to their normal homes. We'll probably never know exactly what happened, but we're hoping that it won't occur again." The announcer thanked the entomologist and the Serious Education Channel started running a preview of its upcoming series on "Wonders Of The Insect World".

THE EXPLANATION

It has been a while since the insects vanished for almost two months before suddenly returning to their normal habitats. Scientists have examined many theories as to exactly what happened. All of the evidence points to the fact that the insects all somehow migrated to a previously unknown zone at the center of the Earth. How they managed that through hot lava, white hot liquid metals and solid metals defies any theoretical explanation.

The real reason is much simpler than the scientists could dare imagine. What we humans did know was that all insects have leaders within their colony, such as the Queen Bee or Queen Ant. What we didn't know is that the Queens all reported to an Empress of their species, quietly co-ordinating the global activities of their kind. Those Empresses all reported to the Grand Empress, who lives at the center of the Earth in the hitherto Unknown Zone.

For some reason, the Grand Empress, who goes by the name of Isabell, had summoned all insects to a Grand Insect Convention in the Unknown Zone. We have no idea what happened there and only have this partial information after a very learned ant accidentally revealed the event whilst playing with a miniature videocamera.

It presumably went well as everything has since proceeded as normal. However, it may be coincidental that a worldwide ban on insecticides, starting with those that hurt bees and ladybugs, has been put into effect. So, **if** the insects were plotting to overthrow the human species, there is no longer a need. We have learned to live together.

THE END

ABOUT THE AUTHOR

Red White

The author was going to use the last name "Wight", after the name of the island in England where he was born - the Isle of Wight.

He then chose the first name "Red" in honor of the Red Funnel ferries, which take cars and passengers to and from the island.

When he considered the pen name "Red Wight", he decided that "Red White" was an easier name for people to remember. It's also a play on the name of a distant family member - Fred White.